D0323893

My Sister, My Friend

My Sister, My Friend

Bonnie Louise Kuchler

☰ WILLOW CREEK PRESS®

© 2014 Bonnie Louise Kuchler

All Rights reserved. No part of this book may be reproduced or transmitted in any form by any means, electronic or mechanical, including photocopying, recording, or by any information storage and retrieval system, without written permission from the Publisher.

Published by Willow Creek Press, Inc.
P.O. Box 147, Minocqua, Wisconsin 54548

Photo Credits:

p2 © Corbis/age fotostock; p6 © Thorsten Milse/Robert Harding Picture Library/age fotostock;
p9 © Gary Randall/KimballStock; p10 © Eric Baccega/NPL/Minden Pictures;
p13 © Donald M. Jones/Minden Pictures; p14 © Servey Gorshkov/Minden Pictures;
p17 © Jane Burton/NPL/Minden Pictures; p18 © Klein-Hubert/KimballStock; p21 © Ron Kimball/KimballStock;
p22 © Rob Reijnen/Minden Pictures; p25 © Manoj Shah/age fotostock; p26 © Ernie Janes/NPL/Minden Pictures;
p29 © Stephen Belcher/Minden Pictures; p30 © Gary Randall/KimballStock;
p33 © Anup Shah/NPL/Minden Pictures; p34 © Labat-Rouquette/KimballStock;
p37 © Labat-Rouquette/KimballStock; p38 © Lisa Hoffner/NPL/Minden Pictures; p41 © Cyril Ruoso/Minden Pictures;
p42 © Charlie Summers/NPL/Minden Pictures; p45 © Carole Walker/NPL/Minden Pictures;
p46 © Donald M. Jones/Minden Pictures; p49 © Luciano Candisani/Minden Pictures;
p50 © Wild Wonders of Europe/Shpilenok/Minden Pictures; p53 © John Short/Design Pics/age fotostock;
p54 © Gerry Ellis/Minden Pictures; p57 © Brian Kimball/KimballStock; p58 © Donald M. Jones/Minden Pictures;
p61 © Tim Fitzharris/Minden Pictures; p62 © Mitsuaki Iwago/Minden Pictures; p65 © Labat-Rouquette/KimballStock;
p66 © Anup Shah/Minden Pictures; p69 © Mark Taylor/NPL/Minden Pictures;
p70 © Klein and Hubert/Minden Pictures; p73 © Klein-Hubert/KimballStock; p74 © Jan Vermeer/Minden Pictures;
p77 © Mitsuaki Iwago/Minden Pictures; p78 © Mark Taylor/NPL/Minden Pictures; p81 © Ron Kimball/KimballStock;
p82 © Richard Wear/Design Pics/age fotostock; p85 © J. Harrison/KimballStock;
p86 © Elmar Krenkel/Lithium/age fotostock; p89 © Scott Stulberg/Corbis/age fotostock;
p90 © Eric Baccega/NPL/Minden Pictures; p93 © Gary Randall/KimballStock;
p95 © Lisa Hoffner/NPL/Minden Pictures; p96 © Gary Randall/KimballStock

Design: Donnie Rubo
Printed in China

For Laura & Leslie,
in memory of the missing part of their heart—
Meredith.

Special thanks to Mary, Vanessa, and Rose,
for giving me a glimpse of your sisters through your eyes.

As sisters, we share an intimate and irreplaceable history.
As friends, we share our most embarrassing secrets.

As my sister, you stay when everyone else leaves, because you need to.
As my friend, you stay because you want to.

Some sisters never cross the bridge from family to friend,
and rarely do friends cross the bridge into family.
So sharing history and secrets and time with a sister like you
is an indescribably precious treasure.

You are my sister, and you are my friend.

A sister is someone you can do anything—or nothing—with.

You never look down on me,

yet you watch over me.

You don't walk in front of me,

yet you lead me home when I get lost.

You don't get underfoot,

yet somehow when I tumble,

there you are to cushion my fall.

$\mathcal{H}$aving a sister is like having a best friend you can't get rid of. You know whatever you do, they'll still be there.

—Amy Li

Sisters are people we practice relationships on,
we practice life on.

$\mathcal{N}$o one knows me the way you do.

People see different sides and hand-picked parts of me,

but you have seen every side and every part.

$\mathcal{B}$oth within the family and without,

our sisters hold up our mirrors:

our images of who we are

and who we can dare to become.

—Elizabeth Fishel

Sometimes one sister looks like Dad and one looks like Mom.
You can't tell they are sisters until they smile,
when their faces crinkle in the same places.

We helped shape each other—
Pushing, pulling, pressing, and pinching,
until our likes and dislikes were formed,
until the glue between us had set.
Until our bond became indestructible.

Siblings are the people...

who teach us about fairness and cooperation

and kindness and caring—

quite often the hard way.

—Pamela Dugdale

Sisters who share a bedroom learn
about basic human needs...
like the need for personal space,
and the need for unconditional love.

A sister doubles your wardrobe, halves your pain.

$\mathcal{M}$any years go by,
and then it dawns on us:
$\mathcal{A}$ little bit of something *with* a sister
is better than a lot of anything by yourself.

$\mathcal{W}$ith sisters, community property can mean
shoes, clothes, French fries, toothpaste,
and of course parents.

My mother's goal was to raise pure, untainted children...
For my sister and me, breaking the rules
was the superglue that held us together.

—Andrea D'Asaro

$\mathcal{W}$e were our own country,
with our own language and songs and dances.
No matter what, my sister will always be my homeland.

If sisters don't make a sound,
they still communicate—
with sideward glances, eyebrow
flicks, shrugs, hugs, twitches, grimaces,
clenches, smirks, and smiles.

You listen in a way no one else can.

You hear me, even when I can't say the words out loud.

Sisters read each other's body language fluently,
which makes it difficult to lie to each other.
It would be like pointing up and saying, "down."

Sisters understand each other in context,
the way people understand nuances of
a word in the middle of a story.

In the language of sisters, "Leave me alone!" really means "Never leave me."

—Katherine Mariaca-Sullivan

A sister smiles when one tells one's stories—
for she knows where the decoration has been added.

—Chris Montaigne

What's the good of news if you haven't a sister to share it?

—Jenny DeVries

I can't hide from you.
When *I* retreat into silence,
you know where to find me.
And you know the way home.

Sisters care more about each other than about censoring their own comments. They risk advice others wouldn't dare offer.

There may be tears, but they will always be washed away by laughter.

—Carol Thomas

*W*hen you hug me,

it feels like a lifetime of love in a single squeeze.

$Sisters...$ hold our hands through the scary parts.

—Ashley Rice

Sisters annoy, interfere, criticize. Indulge in monumental sulks, in huffs, in snide remarks. Borrow. Break. Monopolize the bathroom... But if catastrophe should strike, sisters are there. Defending you against all comers.

—Pam Brown

$\mathcal{W}$hatever separates us has less power over us than

...each other's heart.

—Jacqueline Schiff

$\mathcal{E}$ven the best of sisters have the worst of days.

Our siblings push buttons that
cast us in roles we felt sure we had let go of long ago—
the baby, the peacekeeper, the caretaker, the avoider...
It doesn't seem to matter how much time has elapsed or how far we've traveled.

—Jane Mersky Leder

Sisterhood is a bond woven of fights and forgiveness, and of threads that connect straight to the heart.

Our similarities feel like home—
a place to relax.
But our differences push us to new places,
to try new things.
Can you imagine all the things
I would never have tried
without you as a sister?

Sisters set their course and steer by each other.
Together they find true north.

There is no outsider anywhere who wouldn't appreciate and even envy the tremendous advantage that sisters have, if properly utilized, against all odds.

—Susan Ripps

Most people want at least two feet of personal space between themselves and the next person.

But not sisters.

They are practically an extension of each other.

A sister can be seen as someone who is both
ourselves and very much not ourselves—
a special kind of double.

—Toni Morrison

With fresh eyes we peered from the window,
and together caught the light on the world at the same angle.

Or so I thought,
until I heard your version of my memories.

It seems our window was more a kaleidoscope,
turning slightly between us, and
shifting all the lighted pieces.

$\mathcal{I}$ have been given the wonderful gift of a kindred spirit.

—Marci

Memories were not something we tried to make;
yet in my most vivid recollections, you are there.
We explored life together before we knew that memories were treasures,
more collectible than dolls and rings.

$\mathcal{W}$e were already sisters, already friends,
before we hid behind makeup and clothes and courtesy.

Sisters share a love
made of facets and flaws
and pouts and hugs
and irreplaceableness.

$\mathcal{H}$ow do people make it through

life without a sister?

—Sara Corpening

You know full well as I do the value of sisters' affection to each other; There is nothing like it in this world.

—Charlotte Brontë